THE José Carreras COLLECTION

Aquellos Ojos Verdes 28

Cançó De Passar Cantant 50

Cançó Incerta 41

Canticel 36

El Cant Dels Ocells 3

Festeig 38

Júrame 12

La Partida 54

Maig 46

¡Maitechu Mía…! 20

Morucha 24

Te Quiero Dijiste 32

Valencia 8

Wise Publications
London / New York / Paris / Sydney / Copenhagen / Madrid

Exclusive Distributors:

Music Sales Limited
8/9 Frith Street, London W1V 5TZ, England.

Music Sales Pty Limited
120 Rothschild Avenue, Rosebery, NSW 2018, Australia.

Order No. AM91348
ISBN 0-7119-3604-8
This book © Copyright 1994 by Wise Publications.

Unauthorised reproduction of any part of this publication by
any means including photocopying is an infringement of copyright.

Book design by Michael Bell Design.
Compiled by Gerry Mooney.
Music processed by New Notations.
Photographs courtesy of Retna.

Your Guarantee of Quality:
As publishers, we strive to produce every book to the highest commercial standards.

The music has been freshly engraved and the book has been carefully designed to
minimise awkward page turns and to make playing from it a real pleasure.

Particular care has been given to specifying acid-free, neutral-sized paper made from
pulps which have not been elemental chlorine bleached. This pulp is from farmed sustainable
forests and was produced with special regard for the environment.

Throughout, the printing and binding have been planned to ensure a sturdy,
attractive publication which should give years of enjoyment.

If your copy fails to meet our high standards, please inform us and we will gladly replace it.

Music Sales' complete catalogue describes thousands of titles and
is available in full colour sections by subject, direct from Music Sales Limited.
Please state your areas of interest and send a cheque/postal order for £1.50 for postage to:
Music Sales Limited, Newmarket Road, Bury St. Edmunds, Suffolk IP33 3YB.

Printed in the United Kingdom by
Caligraving Limited, Thetford, Norfolk.

El Cant Dels Ocells

Traditional. Arranged by Robert de la Riba.

© Copyright 1966 Robert de la Riba.
This Edition © Copyright 1994 Union Musical Ediciones S.L.
All Rights Reserved. International Copyright Secured.

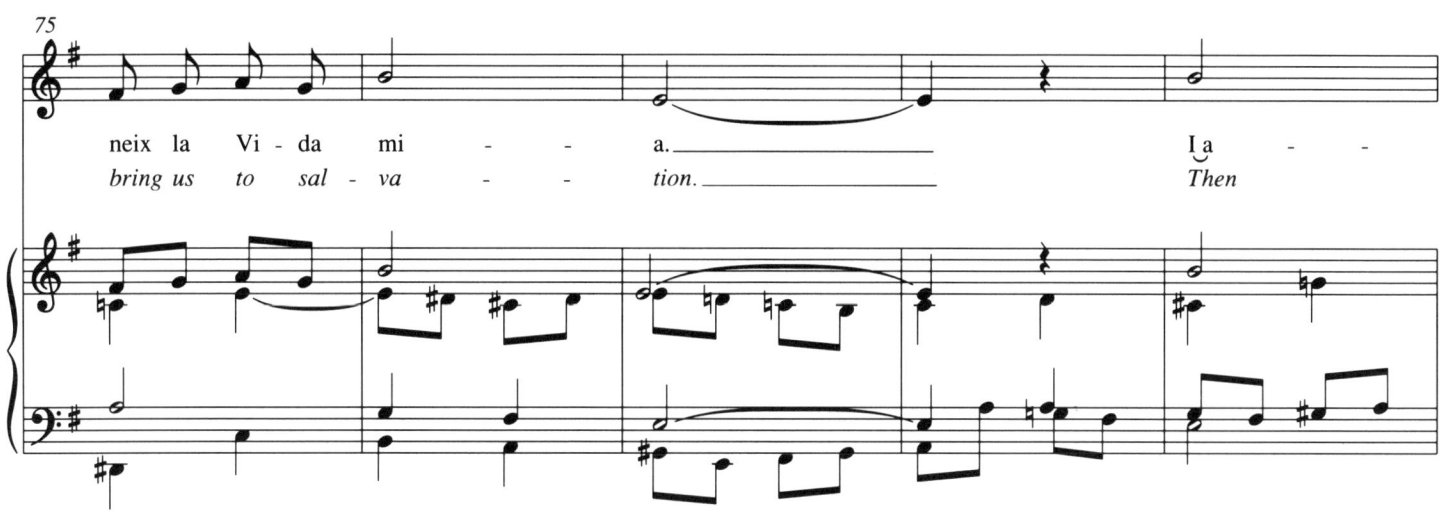

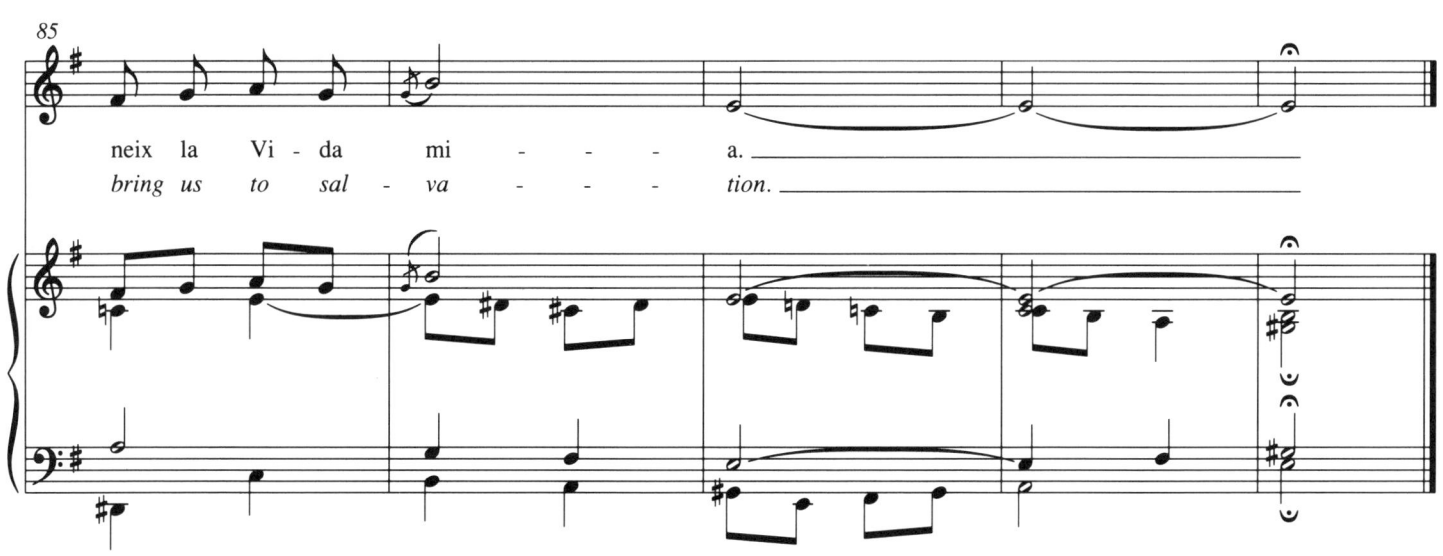

Valencia

Music by José Padilla. Original Words by Lucien Boyer & Jacques Charles.
English Words by Eric Valentine.

© Copyright 1926 Editions Salabert, France.
Sub-published by B. Feldman & Company Limited, 127 Charing Cross Road, London WC2H OEA.
All Rights Reserved. International Copyright Secured.

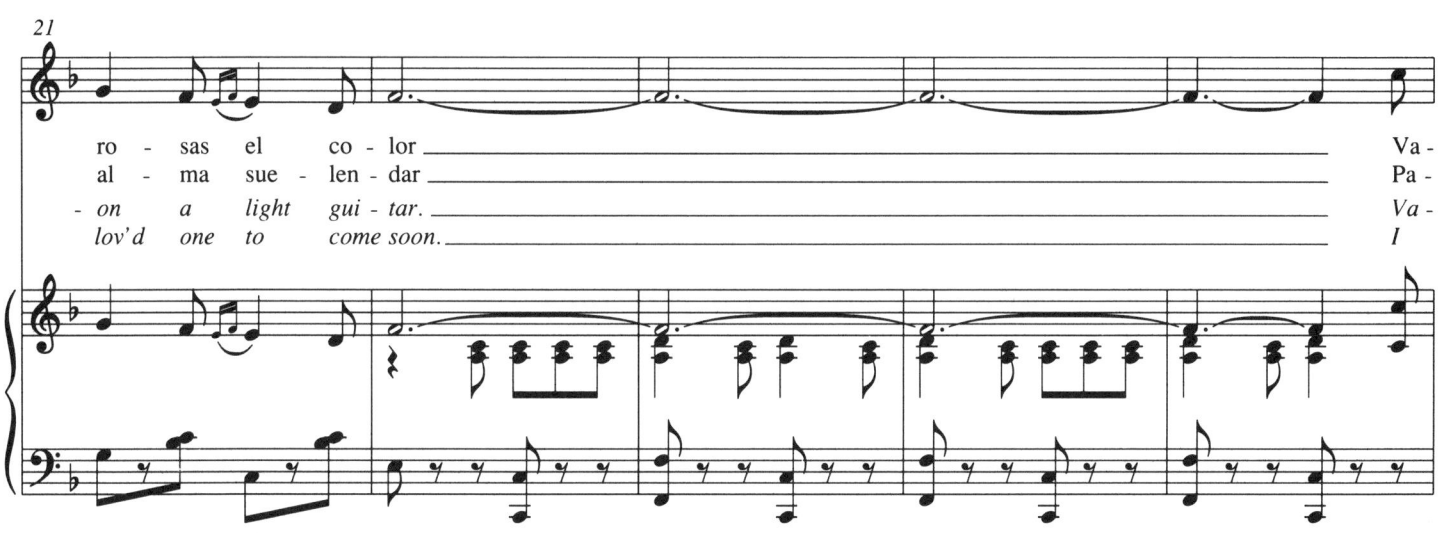

Júrame

Music & Original Spanish Words by Maria Grever. English Words by Frederick H. Martens.

© Copyright 1926 G. Schirmer Incorporated, USA.
All Rights Reserved. International Copyright Secured.

Amapola

Words by Albert Gamse. Music by Joseph M. Lacalle.

© Copyright 1924 Joseph M. Lacalle.
© Copyright assigned 1933 Edward B. Marks Music Corporation, USA.
Campbell Connelly & Company Limited, 8/9 Frith Street, London W1.
All Rights Reserved. International Copyright Secured.

¡Maitechu Mía...!

Music by Francisco Alonso. Original Spanish Words by Emilio G. del Castillo.

Morucha

Music by Juan Quintero. Original Spanish Words by Juan Garcia.

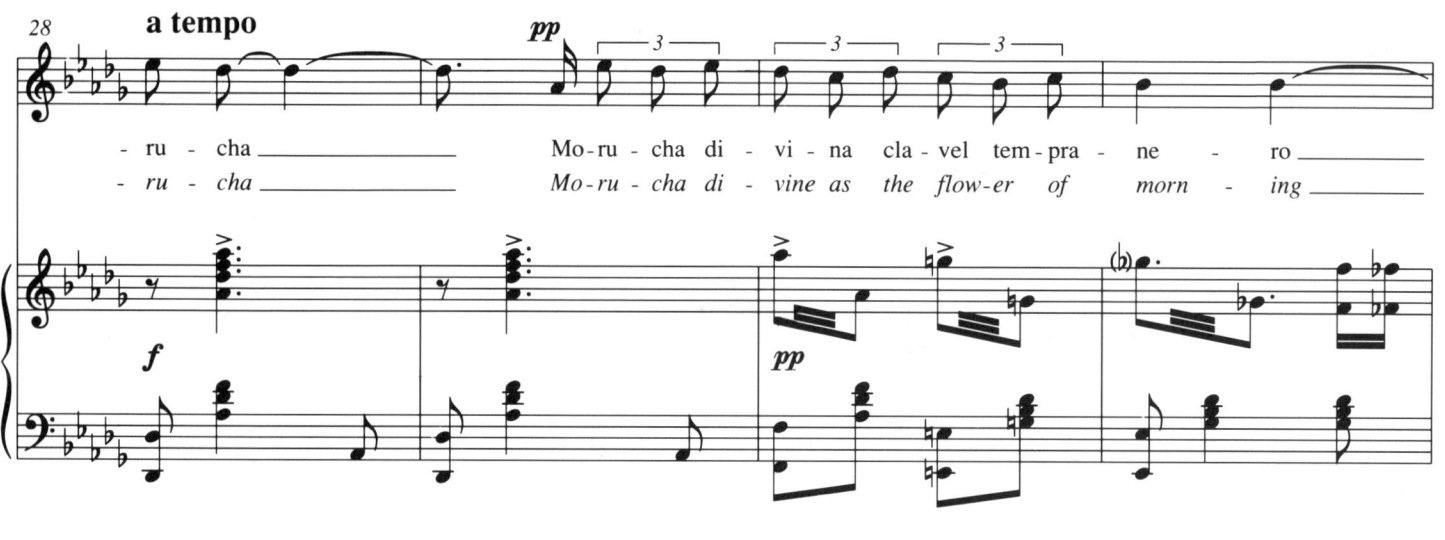

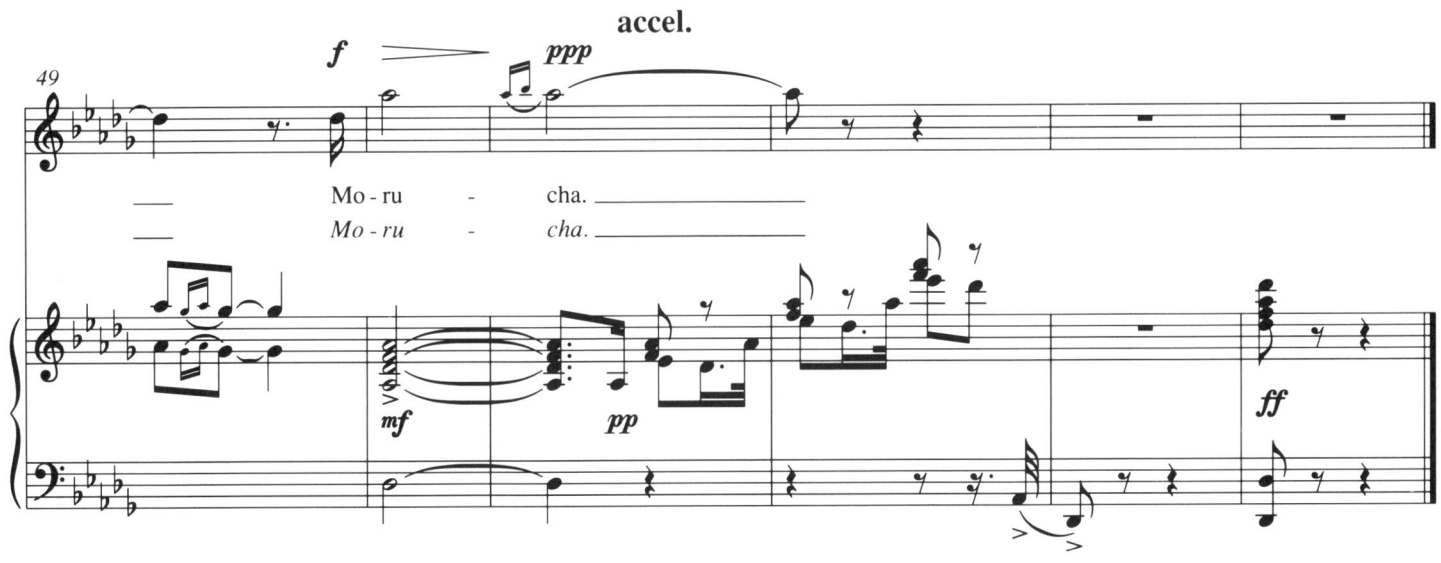

Aquellos Ojos Verdes

Music by Nilo Menendez. Original Spanish Words by Adolfo Utrera.
English Words by L. Wolfe Gilbert & Reg Connelly.

© Copyright 1931 Edward B. Marks Music Corporation & Peer International Corporation, USA.
Campbell Connelly & Company Limited, 8/9 Frith Street, London W1 (66.66%)/
Latin American Music Publishing Company Limited, 8-14 Verulam Street, London WC1 (33.33%).
All Rights Reserved. International Copyright Secured.

Te Quiero Dijiste

Music & Original Spanish Words by Maria Grever. English Words by Charles Pasquale.

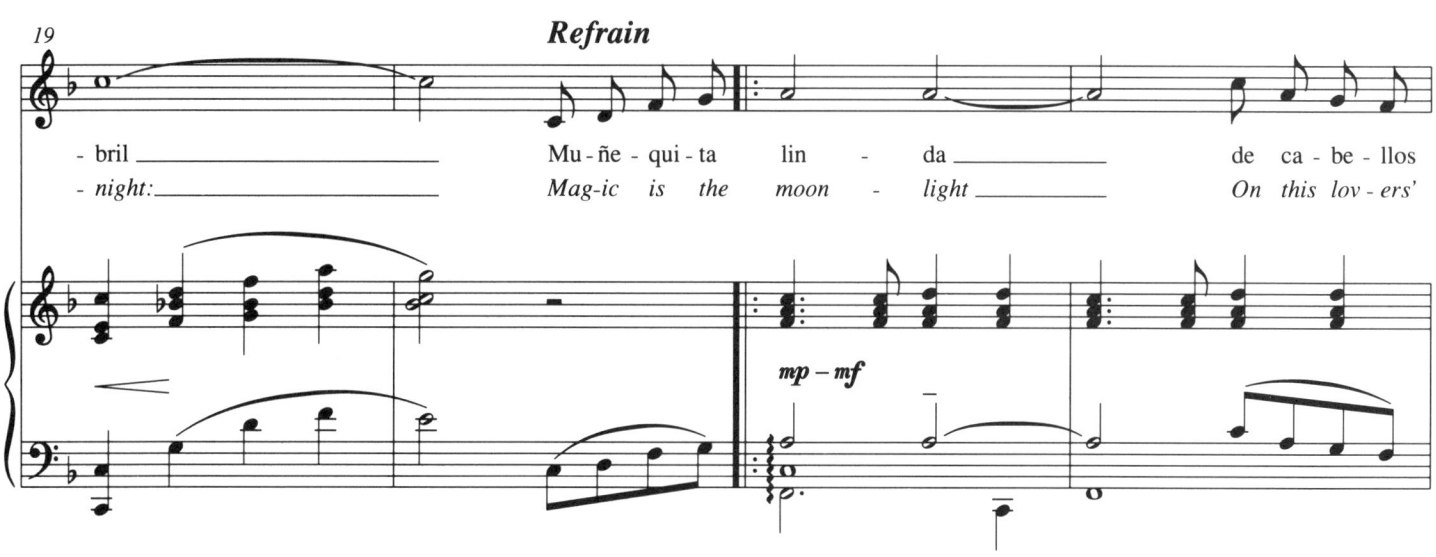

Canticel

Music by Eduardo Toldrá. Original Spanish Words by J. Carner.

Festeig

Music by Eduardo Toldra. Original Spanish Words by J. Maragall.

Cançó Incerta

Music by Eduardo Toldrá. Original Spanish Words by J. Carner.

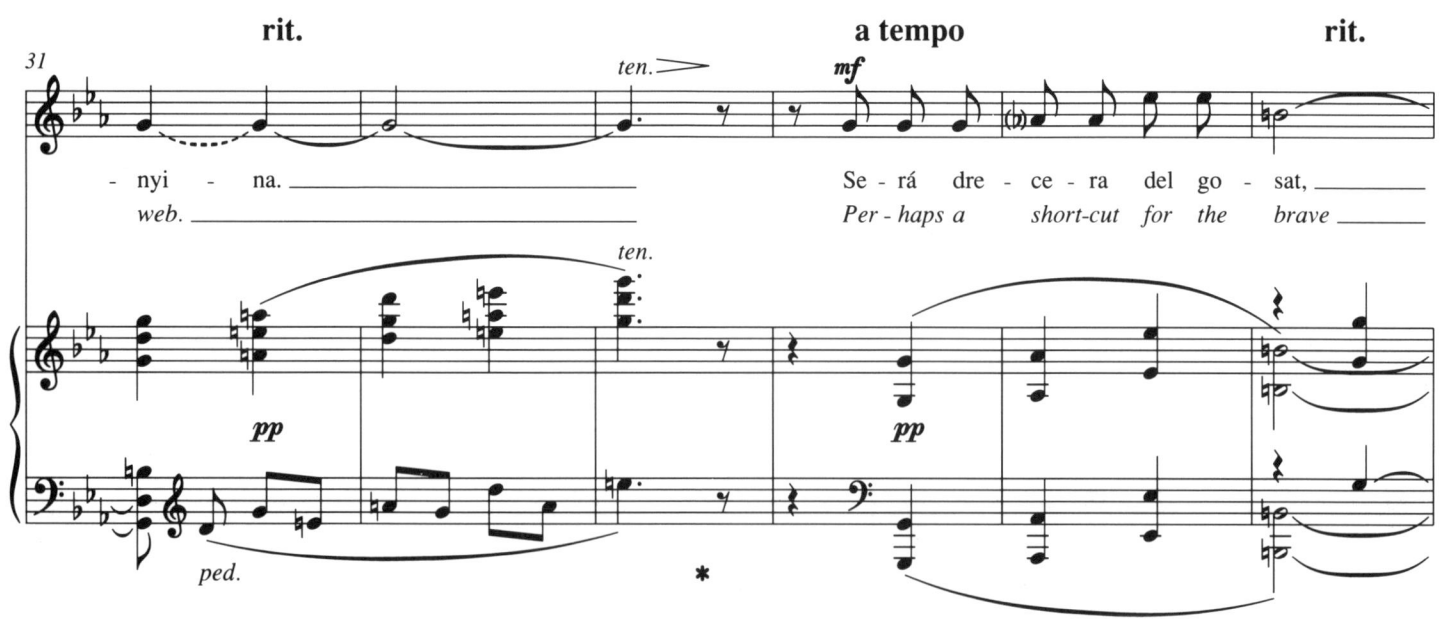

Maig

Music by Eduardo Toldrá. Original Spanish Words by T. Catasús.

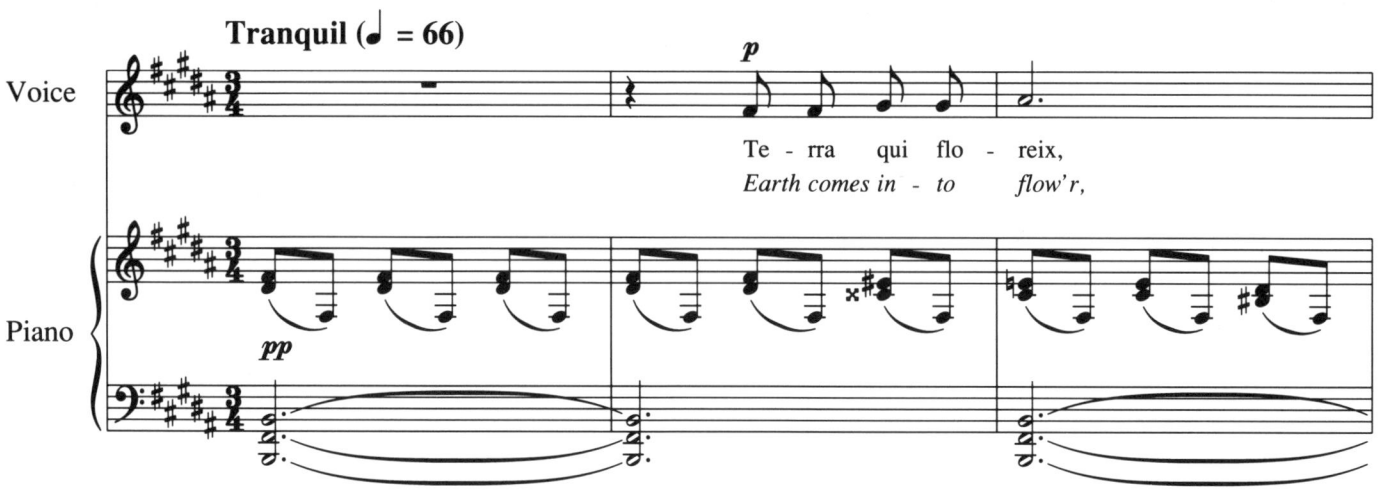

© Copyright 1956 Eduardo Toldrá & T. Catasús.
This Edition © Copyright 1994 Union Musical Ediciones S.L.
All Rights Reserved. International Copyright Secured.

La Partida

Music by F.M. Alvarez. Original Spanish Words by E. Blasco.

© Copyright 1871 F.M. Alvarez & E. Blasco.
This Edition © Copyright 1994 Union Musical Ediciones S.L.
All Rights Reserved. International Copyright Secured.